the
Handbag Book
of Girly Love
Emergencies

First published in 2002

3 5 7 9 10 8 6 4 2

Text © Jacqueline Williams 2002

All rights reserved. No part of this publication may be reproduced, stored in a retrieval
system, or transmitted in any form or by any means, electronic, mechanical, photocopying,
recording or otherwise, without the prior permission of the copyright owner.

First published in the United Kingdom in 2002 by Ebury Press
Random House · 20 Vauxhall Bridge Road · London SW1V 2SA

Random House Australia (Pty) Limited
20 Alfred Street · Milsons Point · Sydney · New South Wales 2061 · Australia

Random House New Zealand Limited
18 Poland Road · Glenfield · Auckland 10 · New Zealand

Random House South Africa (Pty) Limited
Endulini · 5A Jubilee Road · Parktown 2193 · South Africa

Random House UK Limited Reg. No. 954009

Papers used by Ebury are natural, recyclable products made from
wood grown in sustainable forests.

A CIP catalogue record for this book is available from the British Library.

ISBN 0 09 188907 3

Designed by Lovelock & Co.

Printed and bound in Great Britain

the Handbag Book of Girly Love Emergencies

Jacqueline Williams

EBURY
PRESS

Acknowledgements

Bob, Claire, Doc, Jacq, Katie, Kate, Jo John, Lee-Anne, Liz, Paula, and Freddie for providing distraction.

About the author

The author is a wine-swilling girly whose social life is all too frequently interrupted by the demands of her job. An expert escapologist and self-professed blagger, she has been around the block a few times and learnt some things on the way.

After growing up in Australia with tolerant parents and two full-on sisters she moved to live in London. Trying out lots of different jobs, travelling, and testing out as many men as possible and finally finding a good one, have all provided the inspiration for the *Handbag Book of Girly Love Emergencies*.

Contents

Unlucky in love? Feeling like you never meet the right man? A beginner to the love game or starting out afresh after a break-up? Or maybe you're in a relationship but the shine is beginning to wear off and you need help?

Whether you're looking for love, sex or just fun, this handbag book is full of sizzling ideas to point you in the right direction. Whatever your situation, I can't promise you a perfect relationship or guarantee that your heart's true love will turn up on your doorstep, but armed with these tips you'll be better prepared for any girly love emergency that arises.

And when you do bump into a gorgeous man you'll be more able to figure out if he's a minger or a honey, honest or dodgy. What's more you'll be so much more confident and clued up, you'll enjoy it more too.

Happy hunting!

On the Hunt

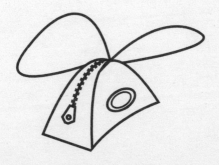

Let's start at the very beginning – if you're single and out there on the scene, it's great fun but every girl can use some extra pointers to really make the most of it. Limber up girls, let the hunt begin.

HELP! I need to know the basics – I haven't got a man and I want to know how to find one

Well, they are everywhere looking cute and tempting but you can't exactly barge up to one, grab his bum and expect a) it to be the start of a beautiful relationship, b) to be sure that he will fancy you or c) that he won't be an utter bore beneath his pretty exterior.

This can be an effective method of pulling if you're in a wild phase and you just want to have fun (and/or illicit sex) – because make no mistake, if you approach a bloke like this he'll think you're fully up for it.

The blatant approach is good to use when you're not looking for a relationship and just want to meet, talk, dance with and seduce gorgeous men, with no strings attached. Because you're not fixed on the outcome, and not too serious about it, you'll find it a cinch to meet men.

Girly dating philosophy

Take a risk, treat it as a game. What is the worst thing that can happen? Rejection isn't so bad if you remember that there are plenty more men where he came from and that life experiences make you a stronger person – if you know you can take life's knocks then you will exude confidence, which is an essential girly quality.

I haven't been in a relationship for ages, and I want a boyfriend not just a casual fling ...

You make plans and set goals for other things in your life, so why not love? Pour yourself a glass of wine and ask yourself honestly what you want in a relationship? Make a list. Think about your past relationships, the things that you liked about them and those you didn't like. You might be more clued up once you're clear about what you want.

Don't discount the men you might already know without considering them.

Have a think about old acquaintances, guys at work, men you know through sports or clubbing. Your taste is constantly evolving so you may fancy someone today who you wouldn't have considered last year. Have you met all of your friends' friends or their brothers and cousins, uncles even? It's about time you supported your friend by going along to that family party she's dreading ...

Girls night-in games

You need: a group of girls, some pens and paper and liberal quantities of white wine and snacks.

Each of you should make a list of the top 10 characteristics of the man of your dreams.

It is hysterically funny the stuff you'll come up with and you'll soon realise how different (and wonderfully shallow) you are from your mates when you put cute bum at the top of your list and they say 'brilliant mind' ...

Breaking all the rules

You don't have to have a boyfriend, you don't have to marry by a certain age or at all, you don't have to move in after a certain length of time. Forget the pressures, have fun and make up your own rules whether you're single or with someone.

Give it your all – let yourself go and enjoy it. Life is not a dress rehearsal, live it now.

What's wrong with me, I just never seem to meet any nice men?

You have to get out – you won't find someone if you're addicted to your sofa. And there's no point moaning about not having a man if all you ever do is go out with the same large group of friends – groups can be quite threatening, making it tough for anyone else to get close.

Imagine being a bloke and seeing you and fancying you but you're with a huge group of friends, scary!

I feel freaked if I go out and all the other girls are drop-dead gorgeous ...

There is a downside to being too good-looking – a lot of time is spent fending off guys you're not interested in. And you'll get guys who are more interested in you as a trophy than as a human being.

Don't forget that not all guys are supermodels either.

Girly attitude

Your attitude to life is a huge part of what people notice about you. It's part of your look so make sure it's positive and upbeat. Fake it sometimes if you really need to and then you'll start to feel it.

Lucky girls

... Create opportunities for themselves.

... Take risks – chat to someone you like when you see them – what have you got to lose?

... Make an effort to go to new places and try new things and you will create your own luck. The more things you do and try, the more men you will meet.

Positive girlys

Say 'yes' to any invitations that come your way – you never know who might be there.

OH NO! – all my friends have boyfriends and I feel really left out

Do you really want a boyfriend or are you just miffed that you're the odd one out?

You don't have to have a boyfriend, maybe it isn't a huge priority for you at the moment; if you're young and carefree (or older but feel young) you don't have to tie yourself down.

Why not just play the field, date and have sexual flings if you like, without hoping that every guy you meet will want a long-term relationship or marriage. That is what most blokes do; they don't feel bad about it and they don't agonise as much as we do about relationships.

I get fed up waiting for blokes to chat me up, so how do I approach them?

Bold girly
Flirty and bold: approach him with the line 'you look thirsty, can I get you a drink, but you'll have to help me at the bar' to get him away from his friends.

What will he think?
Well, if a guy approaches you full guns blazing, really slick and flirty with great chat-up lines, you probably think it's great and a laugh but also think 'I'm not the first woman he's done this to'. He'll probably think you're a seasoned chat-up chick and that's no bad thing.

When does the bold approach work?

It works with most blokes but especially with less worldly or younger guys – they're pretty blown away as it may never have happened to them before. They'll probably be seriously excited by the attention (and relieved that they won't have to cross the room to approach you themselves). And they're probably beside themselves with thoughts of what lies in store.

OR

Subtle girly

You walk past the place that he is standing, look up into his eyes as you pass to the bar or the loo. Repeat the look on the way back and hold the look for a few seconds – you've signalled your interest, now it is his turn to respond.

And when you finally get to talk to him

Relax and treat him like you would a friend and don't get hung up on the 'right' way to behave.

Girly do your own thing

Don't leap into every relationship as if it will lead to an engagement ring if only you can hang on long enough.

There are different types of relationships – short, long, casual, exclusive, long-distance. They're not all about spending every minute together and eventually leading to marriage. You'll enjoy it more if you just relax and see what happens.

It is so frustrating – it's like going out to buy an outfit knowing exactly what I want, having the money and not being able to find it!

What's this about? Having the courage to be a wild sexy beast for the night and then not finding anyone who is up for it.

Some girls can tell as soon as they walk into a room who is up for it. It's no great secret; it is so simple you'll be amazed. You can't be passive, you have to think of yourself as the ultimate vixen out on the hunt – you want to find your match. Look boldly and brazenly around the room, those who are looking for excitement will get a whiff of whatever saucy chemicals you're giving off and look up (that is if they're not already scanning the room), they'll meet your gaze and look steadily and you'll know they're after the same thing as you.

How can you tell if someone is looking for a relationship?

There's no foolproof way to tell I'm afraid but you can exclude all of the guys blatantly scanning the room looking for a bird, they want fast action so avoid them if you're looking for love.

I'm not good-looking enough to attract a guy so what can I do …

Seriously this is a key bit of the mating game where 'act as if' is vital to success. Smile, act confident and chat to people.

Spend some time on your appearance so that you know you look the best you can and then act as if you are gorgeous. You may feel like you're faking it at first, but as you get the reaction you want from men – you'll know you are attractive.

He's a great looking guy, nice personality but crap dress sense ...

Well, you can't have everything. He might be worth trying out for one date – give him the benefit of the doubt, he might be having an off night on the clothes front.

If you do get together, the make or break factor is if he will wear what you tell him to – I know this is something out of the dark ages but if he has all those plus points you gotta hope like hell that you can sort it out somehow.

Don't even go there

Shoes are an entirely different matter. If you hate his shoes, no matter how gorgeous he is forget him.

You won't be able to stop thinking about them – even in the throes of passion. And whenever you introduce him to your mates you just know they'll be looking at them in horror.

Pulling

My mates all seem to pull effortlessly. I get stuck on my own while they chat away ...

Just think of it like you do making friends – if you're interested in talking to someone, you have to give out friendly vibes. If your mates are pulling and you aren't, try to figure out what it is that is so appealing about them – are they friendly, funny, a good listener?

If your mate has the face of Christy Turlington, the bottom of Kylie and the breasts of Pamela Anderson (but real), then you're setting yourself up to be left on your own. The blokes who are obsessed by appearance will swarm round her, making it impossible for other guys to get near you.

Yikes, I've just pulled and he's a right lemon. How do I get rid of him without being a total bitch?

If you've picked the wrong guy don't waste any more time – the fastest and easiest approach is to go to the loo and don't come back. My favourite standby is, 'My mate is here on holiday for just a few days and I've got to get back to her. Nice talking to you.' Change bars if you have to, but get away – life is too short!

Girly pulling gang

Always, always do your man-hunting with chicks of similar rating in looks to you. If you're the plain one, chances are you'll get left on your own; or if you're the more gorgeous, you'll be busy flirting and enjoying the attention of a gorgeous man and behind him your mate'll be lurking, looking stony-faced, and signalling to go home.

Sometimes there are good reasons not to pull

Like when you're not feeling yourself. It's like when you buy a dress when you're fed up – only to find when you cheer up that it just isn't right and you never wear it.

It really is the same with men – if you're feeling down and needy and meet a guy who you think will fix you up, you might not feel the same way about him once you feel better. As for him – he was attracted to you when you were fed up, so he might have a thing about miserable chicks or he's the kind of guy who wants to 'look after you', which can feel suffocating once you're on form again.

Men go for girls who are ...
Naughty, rebellious and opinionated with a devil-may-care attitude, not prissy, affected and obsessed with their appearance.

I meet great guys but things always seem to go wrong, what can I do?

You need the girly where-did-it-all-go-wrong checklist! Tick off the ones that apply to you – there's your answer.

Are you?

- 💔 desperate to hang on to him
- 💔 clingy
- 💔 always waiting for him to call
- 💔 only happy when you are with him
- 💔 prepared to drop everything for him
- 💔 available whenever he wants to see you
- 💔 always hinting that he is 'the one'

Do you?

- 💔 make jealous scenes
- 💔 want to be with him all of the time
- 💔 give up your mates
- 💔 ring him constantly
- 💔 take him for granted
- 💔 expect him to make you happy
- 💔 expect him to sort out your problems
- 💔 snap at him in front of his mates
- 💔 want to change him
- 💔 let him walk all over you

Number one girly dating tip

The most important thing about the dating game is to relax, don't take it too seriously, don't be desperate and have a laugh for God's sake!

HELP! I'm in love with someone who's taken

You may be able to lure him away, but remember if he comes on to you when he is with someone else he might do the same to you.

I'm torn between two lovers, I don't know which one to choose

If you are forced to choose between two guys (you poor darling girl!) go for the personality type you haven't tried before. If you usually go for shy types choose the bolder one. Who knows what will happen if you try the riskier more exciting man for once! If bold is your type, try a shy one – there could be a lot going on beneath that exterior.

Girly don't touch him with a bargepole

Don't go out with anyone who on an early date:

- picks his nose in front of you
- uses toothpicks, obsessively picking food out from his teeth
- slags off his ex
- flirts openly with other women
- scratches or holds his crotch a lot
- looks over your shoulder and around the room when you are together.

Help, I've met someone gorgeous who likes me too, but he's just split up with his girlfriend

If you meet someone who you really, really like and they've just bust up with their girlfriend, you have got to hold yourself back from pursuing him to have any real chance of snaring him.

If you really want him, you need to give him space to make him feel that he is still single – while actually you've reserved him, but he won't know this as you'll be staying cool and slightly distant.

If you can't resist him and want to see and call him up all the time it's time to play a girly game, getting your mates to help you:

Be busy – pretend to be working out of town on a regular basis, go on holiday, visit friends in the country or another city at weekends. In fact do anything to stop yourself pestering him or being available. It is vital that he feels that he is chasing you.

Basically you need to bide your time and make him feel like he is having his freedom until you sense the shine has worn off singles bars and drinking with his mates every night, he's had a break and he is ready to pursue you properly.

Girly loneliness

He's out of town – don't be a wimp – distract yourself and arrange to do some things you really like doing. Make sure you have a life or there'll be nothing of substance for him to fancy.

Help, I'm looking for Mr Right and I won't settle for anything less

Mr Right doesn't really exist – there are many Mr Rights and Mr Wrongs. The fun is in trying them out.

- ♥ lower your standards, perfect does not exist (you're not perfect either)
- ♥ don't take it so seriously
- ♥ check your criteria – is it out of date?
- ♥ try to be a little less rigid, you might find you already know the man for you – love hides in mysterious places

Girly turn-ons:
- ♥ eye contact
- ♥ laughter
- ♥ confidence
- ♥ a sparkling wit
- ♥ playfulness and fun
- ♥ independence
- ♥ a brain

Girly karma-cuddles

What you give is what you get.

If you spend your life mistrusting everyone you meet and being stingy with love and affection you will get nothing more than that in return.

If you want a more loving life give out more love and affection and see how quickly it comes back to you.

FLIRTING

HELP! I'm hopeless at flirting

You don't have to bat your eyelashes like a lunatic or press up against someone like you've never heard of personal space – quite honestly, it is so rare to be properly listened to that sometimes that is all it takes to be a good flirt. Look into their eyes, listen intently – there you go, it's what they've always wanted – they feel like the most fascinating man in the room and they think you're great because you made them feel that way. It's not like you have to act like a surrendered wife and listen to him talking loadsa crap; if you like him, pay him attention like no-one else exists!

The best girly flirt tip
Become adorable and lovable and happy with a positive attitude.

Girly flirt strategies

- 💜 listen intently
- 💜 ask intelligent questions
- 💜 make him laugh
- 💜 ring your eyes with kohl to make them huge
- 💜 lick your lips – occasionally
- 💜 touch your body
- 💜 stand closer to him than you usually would
- 💜 in a loud bar, brush his ear ever so slightly with your lips when you're talking to him

Girly wise-up time

If you haven't got a life get one fast – it's not a good thing to base your life around whoever you are going out with, as you'll be left with nothing each time a relationship breaks up. And no guy likes to think he's got a fatal attraction on his hands.

Txt flirting

You haven't seen him all week and tonight you're going out –
start the flirting early by sending short txt mssgs.

Say:

I'm feeling a bit hot …

Oops – you caught me naked …

I've just stepped out of the shower and I can't wait to see you.

Ask what he is wearing and he is bound to ask you.

Describe your knickers if you dare.

Tell him you are lying in bed and you're thinking of him …

Girly 3-smile attack and you've got him

You're standing in a crowded bar, you've seen him, you fancy him like mad. Get ready to flirt!

1. Catch his eye and smile, look away, count to ten (in your head!)
2. Look at him again, smile and look away.
3. Repeat.

On the third smile you've either captured his interest and he'll come over to chat or else he's out – he's had his chance, now you can re-start your hunt.

If the 3-smile attack doesn't work and you're still smitten but you think he might be unaware (some men are awfully thick when it comes to women) then try the bold approach (p.19) before admitting defeat.

Flirt tips

- 💜 Make eye contact and keep it steady.
- 💜 Touch his arm occasionally when you're talking, accidentally brushing his arm, just enough so that you brush the hairs on his arm – electric!
- 💜 If he touches you back fairly soon then he wants you too. Exceptions to this rule: Latin types, they touch everyone – even their mates and aunties.

Switched-on girly

Flirting is great but you need to know that when you flirt you might get a reaction. Be honest, don't act all surprised if you're doing a work-the-room flirt and a guy takes it seriously and tries to get fresh – you were hinting that you were up for it, so don't be too hard on the boy, just let him know if you're not interested …

What is your romantic story or fantasy?

Chances are it is holding you back and restricting your choice of men – let go of it.

Do they have to have a certain look, be a certain height and have the right job to be the man for you?

You are taking dating too seriously and turning away blokes before they even have a chance – open your mind. You might be surprised! Ask your friends if you doubt this, most of them probably couldn't have predicted who they would end up with.

Girly games

When your car (or bus) pulls up at the lights and the guy next to you is stunning, don't just look away, smile boldly at him. He'll love it. Look away still smiling and just before you drive off look again, long and hard.

How can I tell whether they're a good guy or not?

Take note of the clues – they're usually there early on – don't ignore them:

- 💜 they diss their last girlfriend
- 💜 they're bossy
- 💜 they are unreliable
- 💜 they expect sex straight away and get angry if you don't give it

You've got to set your own standards for how you want to be treated – don't accept bad or inconsiderate treatment.

Consider too that you might be making it easy for them to take you for granted.

Are you?

Too eager and willing ... seeing him any time he calls.

Do you?

Feed him dinner as soon as you start going out with him.

Put up with never going out on a date together, but stay at home in bed or watching TV.

Buy him socks when you've only just met.

Don't make it easy for anyone to take you for granted, demand to be treated well.

Girly mantras

If you need help to stop yourself from calling up a man you're trying to stay away from, you need a girly mantra to brainwash yourself in a positive way. Repeat over and over:

I will not shag him ever again;

I will not call him, or whatever it is that you're trying to stop yourself from doing.

Girly love myth - all men are bastards

The truth is you might be aiding and abetting them. Everyone in this world will treat you as you allow them to. You should show that you are a person who deserves respect - not a victim or a wimp.

If you have been treated badly in the past, don't talk about it. Spend your first date with a new guy, banging on about how badly your last boyfriend treated you and any sane bloke would ask himself, why did you let him treat you like that? (If you haven't asked this question yourself by now, you should have.)

Girly wake up and smell the coffee moment

Sadly, the one consistent thing with any man who treats you badly is that you chose him ... Think about where you went wrong in choosing in the past and use that knowledge to help you to pick more wisely next time.

I'm obsessed with a guy and I'm not sure where I stand with him

You need some girly distraction tactics: book up every evening with friends, find another man to flirt with to boost your ego and to remind yourself you don't need him, to be happy. This will take the pressure off and stop you getting obsessive about him.

A good start is to delete his number from your phone so you can't make that call in a moment of weakness or when you've had too much to drink.

Dating

GOING OUT

Looking good, feeling fine

Get yourself in the mood. There's no point going out on the pull
if you don't feel like talking and feel knackered. Stay at home,
apply a face pack, pour yourself a glass of crisp white wine,
climb into a huge bubble bath – and then have an early night,
amusing yourself before you drop off to sleep.

I'm going out for dinner with a new bloke and I just know that I'll get a huge spot on the day – what can I do?

Set something up with a guy you've lusted after for ages and you will get a spot on the day. It is a law of nature, so don't even bother to try and cheat it – you can't, so be prepared. Here's how:

💜 Drink glasses and glasses of water in the days leading up to the date and eat as healthily as you can too.

💜 Check out the latest spot-covering products – loads have tea tree oil and other ingredients added so that they not only cover up, but they help to banish the spots as well.

Other minor irritations

Cold-sores

The other pre-date nightmare is a cold sore – worse because it curtails kissing. Stop it turning into a throbber by dipping an aspirin quickly in cold water, then holding it to the cold sore for a couple of minutes. Some of the aspirin should melt on your lip – that's fine, it'll be doing its job.

Stubble rash

Had a brilliant night with your man but you don't want the whole office to know that you've been snogging.

Try getting the man to shave a bit more.

If it's too late for that, try Rescue Remedy cream to quickly soothe. Don't use foundation to cover it as it will look dry. MAC Studio Fix is the only product to conceal it

Last-minute girly date pack

Armed with this stuff at work, you'll be ready and willing to go out if he should call with an invite you can't refuse for that very night. Throwing on some spiky-heeled sexy shoes and a strappy top, even with jeans or office trousers, and you will look fab and ready to go. Your pack should include:

- 💜 high-heeled shoes
- 💜 sexy pants
- 💜 jewellery
- 💜 strappy top
- 💜 sparkly eyeshadow
- 💜 clips and ties in case your hair is a mess
- 💜 deodorant
- 💜 a rosy blusher to make you look fresh and perky

- ❤ fake tan – it only takes half an hour to work and will make you look so much better
- ❤ toothbrush and paste
- ❤ deowipes or baby wipes (Superdrug unperfumed baby wipes are great)
- ❤ lip gloss

Lucky pants

Do you always seem to pull when you have a particular pair of pants on? Designate them your lucky pants and never go on the pull without them.

Girly myths exploded

You don't need to try too hard

It would be great if you only met men when you'd spent hours getting ready and were looking gorgeous. But it's not like that, you can have some of the best – and most successful pulling – nights out when you've quickly run a brush through your hair, put on some lip gloss and dashed out for a last-minute drink at your local. It's something to do with being natural and relaxed.

The other weird thing is that you'll be likely to meet different men when you're dressed down.

An added bonus is that if you've got your worst pants on and have hairy legs, you'll just relax and have fun and won't get carried away and jump into bed with them ...

Girly cool, calm and collected

I finally have a date with a guy I've fancied for ages and I really don't want to blow it. Help!

Relax – he is not the only guy in the world – you're there to find out if you like him and if he likes you – it's not a job interview.

Have fun, leave your expectations of finding Mr Right at home.

If it's good – result!

If not – next man, please!

Girly hot-date legs

If you really want to feel smooth and sexy, shave your legs on the day of a date instead of waxing – enjoy the feeling yourself as your silky, satin legs rub against each other and relish the thought of how'll he'll react later when he gets his hands on you.

Dating do's and don'ts

💜 Don't bang on about yourself, your family, your job or your ex all night.

💜 Do be aware of the impression you're giving: if you want to talk saucy and sexy all night, that's fine, but know that he'll probably think you're signalling that you're up for it – and maybe even that very night. That is the way men think. If he is the quieter type, sexy chat might scare him off.

💜 Don't babble like a mad thing from nerves.

💜 Do make sure your shave your legs and armpits and wear some decent knickers.

💜 Don't worry about your looks so much that you aren't able to relax and enjoy yourself.

❤ Do have a drink to relax but don't get really pissed unless you know you can hold it.

❤ Don't tug at your dress, play with your bra straps, obsess about your appearance or wear anything that you feel even vaguely unsure about – your tried and true number that you feel great in is the one to wear.

❤ Do talk about politics and your values and beliefs if you want to – you don't want to wait until date number three to find out that he has a passion for neo-Nazi groups or is a born-again Christian.

❤ Don't waste your time – cut your losses and have an early night if the date is awful.

❤ Do keep on dating and don't get disheartened by a bad one.

When should I return his call if he leaves a message?

You don't have to return his calls immediately – let him wait a bit – after all, you do have a life other than him. (Don't you?)

Don't turn into a phone pest by calling him, leaving a message and then leaving messages all afternoon to find out why he hasn't returned your call. You can turn someone from really keen on you to turned off completely by harassing them and it is sooooo uncool.

But I can't bear the suspense – I met him on Saturday, when will he call?

If he calls the next day he is either very sure of you or very silly – everyone knows you need to leave it at least two days before calling. But he really should call before Wednesday. If you haven't heard by then, he should have a good-ish reason.

Girls can make phone calls!

💜 Don't be a pain in the arse and refuse to call him, leaving him to do all the work.

💜 Do call him if you like him, especially if he paid for the date. Thank him, say it was really nice and that you'll have to do it again soon, this time on you.

Girly keep your cool
– if he says he'll call, never, ever ask 'when'?

He hasn't called me, what do I do?

Girly wake up and get over him if:

he doesn't call

you call him

he doesn't call

you call him

STOP! HE IS NOT CALLING FOR A REASON – he probably doesn't want to speak to you – have some pride girl and give up on him.

Girly txt paranoia

Txt mssgs can also be a surefire way of misunderstanding each other – because they are short they can often be seen as terse. Don't be over-sensitive about it – the test is: would you think it was OK if your mate sent you that message?

Boozy txtng

Do you find yourself frequently wanting to call him and send 2am missives when you're tired and emotional (pissed that is)?

Stop! Get your mates to help you by taking away your phone for the night or deleting his number from your phone.

But txting is OK?

Just because it isn't technically a phone call, don't think you can get away with doing it over and over. Think of it as a phone call and you'll be less tempted.

Sometimes it can be like stalking: he's out with his mates, his phone starts to beep and there you are again, leaving another mssg like a lovesick puppy. You're interrupting his time with his mates. Don't harass him or he'll not be intrigued by you as you want him to be. The whole point about playing a good girly dating game is that you stand back a little to give him the chance to miss you.

Sexy txting
Once you're on intimate terms txting can be very, very sexy … more on this later.

Girly drinking

A little lowers your inhibitions, a lot turns you into a right little raver, more makes you stagger and puke.

It's a sad and unhappy fact that when we need to keep our cool we often start to neck our drinks ... If you're worried about making a fool of yourself with some guy, take it easy on the bevvies. Get your mates to help if they're not too drunk.

It's not surprising that so many relationships go wrong – why on earth do we think we can make a good choice in a bloke after seven vodkas ... But that is often when we seem to meet our men.

I don't get this attraction thing – what does it take to attract a guy?

The secrets of attraction are about to unfold.

It's not just about looks, some girls attract men and others don't.

It's what you give out; what you project. The way you hold your body, your posture, how you talk … all have a huge impact. It's about your attitude to yourself, life and other people.

If you like yourself, others will too. They'll think 'She thinks she's OK' and probably go with your view of yourself.

HELP! I go off men once I've caught them?

You're into girly pursuit: the chase is what you like, not the reality of having a boyfriend. It's fab if you're young and constantly on the pull – why tie yourself down? But you need to find a way to break the pattern before you hit thirty, girl, or you'll always be alone.

If you get desperate hire a therapist, just not a cute one.

Wake up and smell the coffee moments

The relationship that never was:
he was going out with someone else or maybe even married; you never went out to dinner; he didn't introduce you to his friends; he often came over to your house after being out somewhere else or working late.

HELLO! He was never your boyfriend. This is not a relationship, it is a shagging arrangement.

COMING HOME AFTER GOING OUT

Should I take him back to mine?

Where do you feel safest and sexiest? If you feel safe, it's good fun (and more liberating) to go back to theirs. Seeing their gaff can tell you a lot about them and you can make a quick getaway whenever you like.

Staying at his

If you think you might end up staying at his, you'll need to be prepared by having this stuff in your bag; it really won't take up much room:

Out-all-night emergency pack

- ♥ wipes
- ♥ toothbrush
- ♥ pants – a g-string so tiny there's no excuse for not having spares

- ❤ mental note as to where you can quickly buy a new t-shirt en route to work
- ❤ sample size moisturiser
- ❤ contact lens case
- ❤ condoms
- ❤ hair tie
- ❤ small comb
- ❤ make-up
- ❤ perfume
- ❤ deowipes

Dating styles

Stand by for how to unravel the mysteries of dating. You've had a first date, what will happen next? It helps to figure out what kind of dater he is:

Good-time boy

You go out, you have a fantastic time – talking and laughing all night. Yet you never hear from him again – what went wrong?

Either he thinks of you as a mate not a date or he has that much fun with everyone he knows. The confusing thing is that if you bump into him, he'll be really pleased to see you.

Don't waste too much time thinking about why he hasn't called. He just doesn't want a girlfriend.

Love-struck

He instantly assumes that one date means that you are boyfriend and girlfriend and seems set to follow you to the ends of the earth. Aaagh!

The thrill of the chase

He'll take you on as many dates as he needs to, charming you all the way, until he thinks he's 'got' you and then he'll stop calling and move on to the next conquest.

Romeo/lover boy

He dates someone new every night – he's looking for his next date over your shoulder as he sits with you.

The total bore

Talks about himself non-stop. That's your cue to nip to the loo and vanish.

The boy for you

You have a great laugh, have loads in common and he is gorgeous!

Quick, ring your mates, you'll need their help to get you through until he rings you to fix another date.

Girly get real - coded invitations - times have changed

Coming in for coffee hasn't meant coffee in a long time …

A drink in their hotel room isn't just a drink – if it ever was …

Both of these things mean taking it to the next level – don't go if you want to stay on the base you're on. But if you want to move on up a base, give a sexy wink and say 'I'd love a "coffee"!'

If he then offers just a coffee without making a move, he is probably sweet but clueless. Get ready to make your move!

Help, we're going on our second date and now I'm really nervous because I know I like him ...

He's called, you're meeting up. You've both passed the first date and you like each other enough to do it all again. Well done!

This is the point at which you should really relax and enjoy yourself but wait, make sure you don't get too comfortable yet. You need to keep your wits about you so you can decide what you really think of him. Get him out somewhere with harsher lighting, try and read between the lines of what he says, get your mates to sit secretly at the next table. You need to be sure before you go any further if he is a loser!

I'm confused – when does dating cross over to relationship?

You've had three dates and ring each other every couple of days: it sounds like you might be heading for boyfriend/girlfriend status, but you still can't be sure. Hold tight for a bit longer and see how it goes.

Don't be afraid to suggest ideas for meeting up. It's when you both start to assume that you'll keep time free for each other on the weekends that you can really start to call him your boyfriend.

You've been on a date, you think he is great and he says he will call

Never wait around for a guy to call – seriously, make sure you've got something arranged – go to the cinema, go to a friend's house and agonise there away from your phone.

It is driving me crazy trying to figure out if he fancies me or not. How can I tell?

- 💜 He pays attention to you – more than he gives to others.
- 💜 He smiles when he sees you.
- 💜 His face lights up and you just know!

He doesn't seem to fancy me – is he just playing it cool?

The catch – he could be playing it cool. Step up the flirting before you give up on him.

The double catch – some of us girls kid ourselves that he is playing it cool when in fact he just isn't interested …Don't keep throwing yourself at him if the flirting doesn't work.

Girly 'is he a bastard' test

Do you let him get away with:

- ☐ calling you up when he feels like it
- ☐ not being interested in your life
- ☐ not introducing you to his friends
- ☐ doing what he wants to do all of the time
- ☐ staring at and flirting with other women
- ☐ putting you down
- ☐ criticising your clothes or body

Ticked more than one of these?

Yep – he's acting like a bastard, don't let it go on.

Write yourself out a list this minute of all the behaviour you've put up with in the past and never will again. Put it where you can see it every day.

Girly get tough

Don't let a guy call at the last minute to go out – very occasionally it's fine but don't make it a habit. Accept nothing shorter than two days' notice.

If he calls up late at night after not calling for days (or even weeks) don't invite him over. He'll have more respect and realise you can't be treated shabbily if you tell him to go away, you're busy – and to call you in advance if he wants to see you.

Superficial girly

In the long run looks aren't the important thing, so take another look at that great fun guy who you don't fancy only because he isn't breathtakingly gorgeous. Once you get to know someone, how they look is just a part of the whole package.

How can I stop blokes treating me badly?

Most guys don't set out to treat a girl badly, it's more a case of being too lazy to behave well because it requires effort. Behaving badly is much easier: not bothering to call when he says he will, blowing you out at the last minute, never bothering to pick up flowers on the way over to see you, forgetting your birthday. All these things make his life easier in the short term – that is, if you let him get away with it. If he starts to behave like this – tell him he can't and don't accept it. Sure, give him another chance if you think he'll change but if you keep giving him chances and he keeps blowing it – the two of you have set a pattern.

Ouch, I keep getting hurt in love – how can I protect myself?

Don't give it all up for him, you need to retain an air of mystery. You can't do that if you tell him everything, spend all of your time with him and always share everything. You are still an individual and the only thing that you can guarantee in this life is that you will be there for yourself – so invest in you. The side effect is that having a life of your own makes you more attractive anyway – watch the men swarm.

I have no problem attracting a bloke, but how do I keep him?

We're pretty basic animals really and we all like a good chase.
Here's how to keep him after you, once you've got his interest:

- ♥ Don't always be available.
- ♥ Don't pursue him endlessly, always wanting to be with him, suffocating him.
- ♥ If he can't always have you when he wants you, he'll be happy because he'll be in pursuit and be keener and want more of you.

Why can't I go for a 'nice' man for a change?

How many magazine articles have you read telling us that we girls don't like 'nice men'. We mistakenly call men who are really keen to the point of being suffocating 'nice' – this isn't nice, this is just dumb. If your man starts to rely on you too much and gives up his life wanting to be with you all of the time and hang out with your friends – tell him to keep a hold of his life.

The truth about nice men

Nice men are men that are honest and straightforward and don't mess you around.

If you're used to guys who play games and toy with you, you might feel bored because you can relax and not spend your life in a state of agitation and hysteria; because you're not always trying to figure out if they like you or why they're behaving as they are.

Forget that – train yourself out of needing angst to feel 'in love'.

He's got a girlfriend – what shall I do?

You've got a choice:

Have fun with him if you want, but don't assume that he will leave her.

If you sleep with him when he tells you he's taken, he'll probably think that means you accept it that way – why would he need to leave her – he's got you both!

OR

You could have your cake and eat it too – that is, if you don't want him full-time then this set-up is actually ideal. Trouble is, it's when you're really not that keen to have him around all of the time that the magnetic effect exerts its pull. He'll probably suddenly be really keen and want to dump his girlfriend for you.

There is always a reason why he can't leave his girlfriend for me. I really love him – what can I do?

There are no 'reasons' only excuses – be a mug and stay with him if you must, but don't make it worse by kidding yourself too. Be aware that your friends are talking about you behind your back, they're bored with you banging on about him constantly and they think you're crap for putting up with it.

Wake up and smell the coffee moments

- He gives you clues all the time but you just won't take the hint.
- When you met him he was singing 'I'm wicked and I'm lazy'
- He thinks it is okay to chat other women up in front of you ...
- And he often disappears half way through the evening and doesn't bother to explain where we got to
- His friends don't seem to know who you are ...

Give it up!

Sex

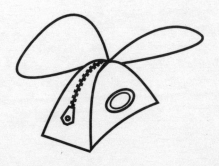

This is the bit where we get down to girly sex, but before we do let's deal with a couple of questions such as:

Does size really matter?

Yes of course it does.

And

Am I frigid?

No - he just needs to try harder to please you.

Read on for girly sexpert tips, hints and other mad advice.

Tell me what sexy girls do?

Sexy girls:

💜 have vodka in their freezer ready to take to bed for a session

💜 keep a sarong on the back of the door for tying on halter-neck style when a man stays – it is sexier and more flattering than dashing about naked

💜 hide their dressing gown

💜 sleep on satin pillows so that they don't wake up with bed hair

💜 have gorgeous – and clean – bedlinen

- keep fags in their bedside drawer for a post-coital smoke (even if they don't smoke)

- never wear pyjamas

- paint their toenails red, even in the depths of winter

- occasionally take their phone off the hook to stay in and pamper themselves – it'll drive him crazy wondering who you're talking to.

Txt sex

Txting sexual innuendos is the ultimate way to get him gagging for you. You can tease, tantalise and hint at all of the delights to come.

We slept together, so he must like me and want to see me again ...

Sorry, but sleeping with you is no guarantee - cruel to say, but he may just have felt horny and you were the closest, cutest thing around. If it's any consolation he liked you at the time ...

How can I make sex even more exciting?

Have fun and don't take it too seriously is the answer - really stay in the moment (almost like meditating if you've ever tried it). Keep your mind off other things - how you look, work, shopping, etc. Tell him what you like the most, focus on how great it feels and tell HIM so. If you spend the whole sesh worrying about boobs, bum or any other bits, you're tuning out from what is actually happening and that detracts from the whole experience.

Sometimes I'm so knackered, I'm really slow to warm up but really love it once we get going – any ideas?

Get yourself ready for a session in advance and spend as much of the day thinking about what you'll get up to without losing your job.

Flirting by txt is a brilliant way to steam things up.

Daydream about all the times when you've had brilliant sex. Fantasise.

If all else fails and you're still not totally horny, get him to totally indulge you with loadsa foreplay.

I've forgotten how to seduce a man – give me some hints

Get him revved up during the day, so that by the time you meet him later that night he'll be ready for you.

Ring him at work and tell him you were thinking of him when you were in the shower and then when you were getting dressed and you can't wait to see him tonight.

Practise undressing saucy style – peel off your clothing slowly and deliberately rather than just taking it off.

More txt sex

If you're really into him, txt him this:

i hUJOH 05 W,I
35V37d 3W
d73H

If he doesn't get it, tell him to turn it upside down.

Sexual fantasies

Are they normal? Are they safe? Will my mum find out?

Fantasising is normal and natural and good for getting you excited.

Talk to your mates about them after you've all had a few drinks - instead of feeling ashamed of yours, you'll probably feel disappointed that your fantasies are so tame!

Lots of girls like being tied up or tying someone up - go girl, if that's your thing, but make sure you trust him before you go there.

Girly warning - you might find that you become overly reliant on those fantasies - addicted even - and you get carried away inside your own head rather than focussing on what is happening in real life.

Dare I tell him my fantasy?

Pick your time to tell him, your gut feeling should tell you
whether he'll be comfortable with it or not. It is very sexy if
you get it right and share your fantasy – who knows, he might
be dying to make it come true.

Does he have a fantasy that you could make come true?

Choose your moment and ask him – be prepared to grab your
bag and make a run for it if it is truly grubby and weird!

Txting foreplay

If you're out, build up the excitement for later by sending him a
one-word mssg – choose words he'll easily recognise that will
remind you of a recent exciting session, or make promises for
later. This is even more exciting if you are in the same room and he
can see you as he reads the mssg.

Passion killers

- ♥ ugly pants
- ♥ hairy backs
- ♥ using rude words in sex before he's checked out if you're cool with it
- ♥ talking about his ex's body
- ♥ barking precise instructions – do this, do that
- ♥ criticising your body – you're supposed to feel sexy after that – I don't think so ...
- ♥ always coming first
- ♥ acting like you're not even there
- ♥ insisting that you spank him when you don't want to (it's a British thing).

How come I always seem to lose my common sense as soon as I'm horny?

'Fizzy' knickers syndrome has a lot to answer for – it can ruin your hearing and eyesight.

It's that thing that happens when you've had a few drinks, you're feeling horny and you get that throbbing, fizzing feeling in your pants and you can't be trusted to use your brain where a gorgeous man is concerned.

How can I combat fizzy knickers?

There are lots of useful 'down girl' devices you can use including:

- 💜 imagining your Gran knowing what you're up to
- 💜 thinking about your favourite pet dying.

How can I be more rational when I'm choosing a bloke?

By all means let the reaction in your pants rule you – take that boy home if you really want to, but don't confuse lust with a careful choice in a bloke. It might sound obvious but what goes on in your pants is not the same as what goes on in your brain.

If you think you suffer from fizzy knickers and you're tired of dealing with the hassle after the fizzing has died down, listen to your friends on this one – they'll tell you if you need to cool down.

Sex in a bottle
Champagne – no scientific evidence but it has to be the best sexual kick-start there is.

Things to make you go oooooo!

💜 breakfast in bed – if he makes it

💜 bubble baths together

💜 swimming naked in the sea

💜 you and him naked and covered in baby oil, writhing on a sheet of plastic (your Twister mat will do – just remember to clean it b4 you next get pissed with your mates and want to play)

💜 a body scrub with some sea salt, finished off with a plain yogurt wash-down in the shower – sounds weird but it is very sexy and it makes you feel all shiny and new

Clued-up girly
- 💜 knows she should go home alone when she is seriously pissed
- 💜 is not always available
- 💜 doesn't waste time over someone who isn't into her.

S-exercises
- 💜 Wait until he is in bed, put on your cutest nightie and do your exercises on the bedroom floor before getting into bed – he won't be able to resist you.
- 💜 Do your pelvic floor exercises – they're not just for ladies who've had babies. Squeeze 'em tight to firm them up and make sex more thrilling and snug for both of you.

How can I make sex better for me?

Being confident about your body is the key – if you're constantly worrying about bulges, how your bum looks, if your boobs are too droopy, you are hardly going to be able to relax and enjoy the moment. Thinking about how your body looks won't change it (get down to the gym if you're that bothered), so why not try and forget your wobbly bits and focus instead on how good you feel and what he is doing to you. He fancies you as you are.

(Let's face it, when he's hot to trot he's not looking at your flabby bits, he's in passion mode and you are the object of his desire!)

Help! How can I keep him interested?

Listen to what he says – maintain eye contact with him when he talks, especially when there are other people present. Make him feel like he's the most interesting person in the room. At the same time, don't be too wrapped up in him. This shouldn't be too hard if you have a life, but if you've given up your mates and want to see him every night – chances are he'll get bored with your constant availability.

Help! I've got cystitis

Otherwise known as honeymoonitis – you know you've been busy at it when you get this. Keep some Apis, a homeopathic remedy in the cupboard along with some bicarbonate of soda (really cheap). Drink a teaspoon full mixed with water to stop your pee burning. Keep cranberry juice in the cupboard (it doesn't go off until you open it) and drink litres of it when you're in a passionate phase to ward off attacks.

Yawn – we're in a sexual rut – help!

Quickies are it!

They can be great fun, make you feel naughty and are even more important to do once you've been together a while. There's nothing like it to make you feel passion anew and get out of a rut.

Sexual healing, it's good for you

💜 Orgasm triggers your body to release endorphins which are brain chemicals that produce a sense of euphoria.

💜 Think of it as a bonus workout, especially if you get on top – your thighs will thank you.

> *Girly go for it*
> Get into the habit of having sex often – the more you have, the more you want, the better it gets.

Help! I'm smitten by a crazy, irresponsible boy – how can I change him?

Don't expect love alone to change him or tame him. You'll drive yourself, and him, mad if you think you can. Accept him as he is or leave him alone.

Oh no, another rainy day!

Have a picnic in bed:

Make loads of yummy finger foods to suck and nibble. Try feeding each other tiny sandwiches and crudités with dips, followed by berries, ice cream or chocolate mousse. Drink fizzy wine or vodka, depending on your mood.

ONE-NIGHT STANDS

Enjoy! They can really be liberating and fun, but be careful who you choose – tell your mates where you're going.

See it for what it is – a lusty encounter that may or may not turn into something else.

Is it possible for a one-night stand to turn into a relationship?

It might do, but don't expect it to. Don't confuse love with lust – only sleep with him if you'd still feel OK about doing it if you never saw him again.

If you really fancy someone and think you might want a relationship, it might be best to go more slowly because it could all fizzle out too soon.

I had a one-night stand with a guy the other night – he left right after sex – do you think he'll call?

No. And nor do you really, forget him!

I'm really into a guy but he only ever calls at the last minute to meet up – what do you think?

He's using you for when he's got nothing better to do – if he really wanted to see you he'd call in advance.

Wake up and smell the coffee moments

I met him just as the club was closing … Mmm, beware the closing-time sniffer.

He has fun with his mates all night or plays the field and then scouts for a shag to take home just as the lights go up.

Sometimes I get so inflamed by lust I frighten myself and want to jump on the nearest decent-looking man ...

Great isn't it – the only tricky thing is (especially if you're single) that you probably feel your lustiest when you're at your most fertile. That is before and around ovulation. So roughly the week after your period (days 8-15) be extra careful about contraception. If you're going to let lust lead, maybe don't get so pissed around this time, so that you choose someone half-decent and won't have to chew your arm off the next morning to get away without waking him.

Seriously. I really need help to take things more slowly ...

If you think you're easily tempted and you'll not be able to resist him, this might help:

- 💜 don't shave your legs or armpits
- 💜 wear your worst knickers
- 💜 wear tight trousers (harder to get out of – impossible to slip a hand under)
- 💜 meet up during the day for lunch or coffee

If you do go into his bedroom (why?) at least make sure you keep your feet on the floor.

Top 10 sexual turn-offs for him

1   never initiating sex
2   lying still while he does all the work
3   leaping from bed to shower immediately after sex
4   calling some other guy's name when you come
5   mentioning your mother (or his) during sex
6   yawning during sex
7   criticising his performance – faster, slower, no, not like that!
8   filing your nails
9   reading a magazine over his shoulder
10 losing interest after you've come before him (hang on that's men isn't it?)

Rohypnol

It really is out there. If you're in a crowded club or bar, buy only bottled drinks so that you can easily hang on to it when you dance and can keep your finger over the top.

Paranoid? Maybe, but by taking a few simple steps you don't have to worry about being drugged. You and your mates should keep an eye out for each other. If your mate seems pissed, more pissed than she should be on what she has drunk, don't let her out of your sight even if she says she is OK.

Holidays

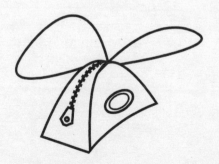

He's asked me to go away with him – I've only known him a few months – what to do?

- 💜 Go for it; just don't make it a long trip around the world.
- 💜 It is probably not a good idea to go away with his mates.
- 💜 A dirty weekend away is a great way to find out more about him and explore every inch of each other.
- 💜 Tricky if you haven't slept together yet and don't know if you want to or not. Assume if you're going away together, he thinks you'll be sharing a room.

Girly homeopath

Buy and take some nux vomica with you on holiday (Boots and healthfood stores stock it). Use it whenever you've overindulged in booze or you're feeling bloated or constipated. Drink lots of water with it and it'll sort you out.

What's the sexiest holiday I could possibly take my man on?

If you've got the time and the cash it has got to be somewhere tropical – what could be sexier than somewhere that you hardly need to wear clothes, where the climate is skin temperature, and where the rain occasionally pours down but only briefly enough to make the atmosphere even steamier. Imagine getting soaked in a warm downpour, and rushing back to your room to peel off your wet things. Or swimming in the sea as the rain pours down, then drying each other off and lying in a hammock together for an afternoon snooze. Thailand, Bali and Malaysia are particularly fab for this kind of holiday and cheap once you get there too.

Dirty weekend kit

- ❤ condoms
- ❤ contraceptives
- ❤ massage oil
- ❤ sexy underwear
- ❤ apis- a homeopathic remedy for cystitis
- ❤ bubble bath
- ❤ bedroom toys

I met a gorgeous guy on holiday, I wonder if we'll ever see each other again?

Enjoy it while you're on hols – you're away from home and can do what you like.

Consider it a bonus if you see each other again after the holiday (that is if you don't already have a boyfriend at home) and a bloody miracle if you actually like each other and can cope in each other's home town. If you end up having a relationship from a holiday romance you deserve a prize!

Girly go-for-it moments

There's no reason not to be wild when …

💜 You're in Thailand, dancing on the beach and you catch the eye of the gorgeous guy who has the beachside bungalow.

💜 You're at a beach bar in Ibiza and you lock eyes with a guy who can really move …

💜 You see someone you're madly in lust with on the last night of your holiday.

Top 10 sexiest cities for a dirty sexy weekend

Rome Eating stunning food, strolling around and people watching – very sexy, but you'll need to dress sharply to keep up with the Romans.

Marrakech Exotic, great smells and sights and gorgeous hotels – bit thin on getting a drink though so stock up on the duty-free.

Venice Romantic gondola rides, sea and atmospheric strolls along the canals. Go easy – it's a place that you could fall in love.

Paris Need we say more. It's a real statement to go to Paris with a lover – all your mates will get it instantly.

Seville Hot sexy days, nights wandering along winding streets to find a Flamenco bar and drink sangria.

Naples Sea, seafood and the mafia. Sexy and dangerous at the same time, a great combination for a dirty weekend.

Barcelona Great for coffee in the mornings (very late), the beach for lunch and a siesta afterwards, and then staying up all night partying.

Dublin If you like your Guinness, atmospheric pubs and a good laugh, Dublin is the place for you. There are a couple of seriously sexy, hip hotels too.

Amsterdam Great fun, chilled-out town but keep away from the coffee shops if you want him to be lively enough for bed action.

Brighton Cheap and cheerful for a shagfest by the sea.

Fazed by those super-cool babes on the beach?

Don't worry it ain't natural – they've been practising. Get
ahead, try on your holiday wardrobe in advance. The whole
point is to look like you haven't made any effort when actually
all you've done is make the effort in advance. Sort out what to
take and what goes best with what – it's really rare to have a
full length mirror on hols and you won't have time anyway. Sort
out your jewellery, practise wrapping sarongs so they seem to
be thrown on effortlessly, and tying flowers, scarves and
headbands for making the most of your beach hair.

Afternoon girly delight

Always, always get your man horny after lunch. Get back to your sun lounger, let your lunch settle a bit and then start your mission to get him hard and back to your room, then a quick shower before slipping between the sheets for a sexy siesta.

Weekend surprise

If he's taking you away on a surprise weekend, not telling you where you're going, make sure you get him to enlist your best friend or sister for help with your packing. You don't want to get there and find you're somewhere seriously stylish with the wrong clothes.

We're going on holiday together for the first time but I snore like a bear. It's so embarrassing – what can I do?

There's a great herbal product to help called Snoreez. It's a blend of oils and vitamins in a spray.

You can also try going to sleep on your side.

Nice but sly girly

If he goes on a trip or holiday without you (bastard!):

Being nice about it can have its benefits – instead of moaning about the glamorous trip your boyfriend is going on (leaving you behind), be nice, help him pack even if all you do is lie on his bed saying yes or no to clothes that he holds up. Get him a book and some sweeties for the flight and tell him to enjoy himself. Tell him all of the plans you have for when he is away.

Have fun and wait for the presents on his return.

SERIOUS STUFF

Don't forget to take condoms with you.

STDs and AIDS are still out there – make it a habit to use condoms, you'll soon find it so easy to do that you can forget about it and be as spontaneous as ever.

Holiday turn-ons

Sex on the beach can be really fab (beware of the sand unless you want sandpaper action – get him to lay down his shirt if you haven't got a towel).

Sex in the water – keep everyone on shore guessing, are they, aren't they? Tie your bikini to your leg so you don't have to emerge naked.

Should I go on hols with my boyfriend or my mates?

Don't take coals to Newcastle. If you're going somewhere where there'll be wall-to-wall men you'd be mad to take a boyfriend unless you're so into him that you won't feel trapped (and envious of your mates pulling gorgeous holiday boys) being with him.

Don't ever go with your mates and your boyfriend unless your mates have got boys with them too.

Don't go with your mates if you are going to bore them silly, moping about missing him the whole time you are away.

Holiday tactics

Wise girlys don't pair up with the first boy they meet – pace yourself, case the place and don't panic and grab one too soon.

If you go to a bar or club, you and your mates have to keep them at bay until you know you've got the cutest boys the resort has to offer.

Stay under cover with your amorous activities – if you're seen snogging too often with too many boys then the horrid boys will think you're up for it with anyone (including yukky old them) and the nice boys will think they're just one in a line (they are but they don't need to know that).

HELP, we can never agree on a holiday – he always wants to do something completely different from me ...

Men can be really weird about planning holidays – the solution is to pick your dream holiday all on your own. Have a night in, get in the brochures, open a delicious bottle of wine, have loadsa gorgeous food on hand and then choose. Next you need to get on to the girlfriend of your boyfriend's most easygoing mate, sell her the idea of the holiday and once they're committed your boyfriend will be easy as anything and eager to go.

Girly give it a miss...

Camping. Unless you're going to keep your hands to yourself, that is, as it is impossible to have a dirty weekend in a tent without alerting the entire camp site.

Then again, it could be fun trying to suppress the giggles and groans.

Caravans actually rock if you do anything more vigorous than play cards. Still they can be a laugh and they are cheap – what do you care if the caravan starts rocking and the walls are so thin that people can hear you having sex?

Relationships

GETTING SERIOUS

Oh no, I've been invited to meet his parents – what if they don't like me?

The golden rule is don't invite them to yours for dinner – you'll have double anxiety over meeting them and your cooking.

Don't put yourself through the agony unless it is really necessary. Only agree to meet a guy's parents if you really need to (like if you're staying at their house) or if you're pretty keen on him. Take some Rescue Remedy (a Bach flower remedy) to help you through. Just relax and be yourself. If you need to drink to calm your nerves, make sure that you choose the booze and the quantity that you can cope with. You might be fine if you stick to G&T, but if you drink champagne you might find yourself flirting with and slapping his dad on the bum before you down two glasses.

Staying in

Help! He's coming over for dinner – what to do?

- If you share, bribe your flatmates to go out
- If you live with your parents, wait until they're away
- Do something simple like grilled chicken or steak with new potatoes
- Open a few bags of salad and throw them in a bowl with some dressing
- Make him feel comfortable and useful – get him to open the wine and find glasses
- Light candles all over the room
- Have some fab and funky music ready – putting on a romantic tune or your flatmate's 'Lady in Red' CD by mistake would really be a passion-killer

💜 Do a quick clean-up

💜 Leave a couple of pairs of saucy pants 'drying' on the bath

💜 Arrange some delicately fragrant flowers – if you're planning that he stay, put some bold red ones in the bedroom

💜 Fragrance in the air – with all that sexiness, if you have some vanilla fragrance, it will add a biscuity home-cooking aroma to the ambience

💜 Shove everything else unsightly into a garbage bag and hide it.

If he is staying over

💜 Drape your sexiest nightie near the bed – as if you've left it there from the night before, not laid out for his benefit

💜 Hide your grubby dressing gown

💜 Make sure he leaves satiated in every way by giving him fresh coffee and croissants in bed.

OR

💜 If you want to send him on his way begging for more, drag him out of bed and down to your local café where you can gaze into each other's eyes over a bacon sarnie. There's nothing more tantalising than wanting to have each other again and not being able to …

Now that you're an item ...

It's easy to blow it all by taking him for granted – think about
it. Are you nicer to, and less prone to be bad-tempered with,
your friends and colleagues? Wise up, so you don't lose him!

- 💜 Do you hold it together all day only to lose it once you
  walk through the door?
- 💜 Do you expect him to make you happy?
- 💜 Do you think it's his fault if you are unhappy?
- 💜 He is a bonus in your life, not there to sort you and your
  problems out, so treat him as if you really want him to
  stick around.

Essential girly bedside kit

- 💜 condoms
- 💜 KY jelly
- 💜 peppermints
- 💜 tissues
- 💜 baby wipes
- 💜 lip gloss
- 💜 a bottle of water
- 💜 baby oil
- 💜 a powder compact to quickly fix your face when he's in the loo

- 💜 And if he's not with you – your mobile if you're expecting him to call and you're planning a sleep-in.

Girly flatshare etiquette

Help, it's impossible to get romantic with my flatmates around …

- 💜 Take it in turns to have nights in alone.
- 💜 Agree to some rules about sex in shared areas – is it OK to do it on the sofa?
- 💜 Have a secret signal, put a pair of knickers or a ribbon on your doorknob to show you've got company.

LOVE

Those three little words – who should say 'I love you' first?

It's not a boy or girl thing, it's about whoever feels braver at the right moment. It'll be fine if you've both dropped pretty heavy hints that you are seriously into each other. Go ahead and say it – if you're sure he won't laugh in your face or recoil in horror.

Don't say I love you:
- 💜 when it's lust – poor boy, he might take it seriously
- 💜 if you've only just met
- 💜 if you have no idea how he feels about you

Does he really mean it when he says 'I love you'?

Don't always take it too seriously if you don't know each other well – after all, they are just three teeny, tiny words. They take no time at all to say and let's face it, sometimes we get carried away in the heat of the moment and before we know it we've said it.

Girly rows

Help, I can't bear it when we row, I get really angry

If you're having a row, don't bring up the past, just stick to what you're arguing about now. Don't sulk and hold a grudge. Remember you do like him. You just don't like what he is saying.

Girly wisdom

Everyone and every relationship has a different lust phase, but just don't get too carried away and fall in love before you've given yourself a chance to get to know him.

Actions speak louder than words

God, how did my mother get in here!

Well, she was right – he can say whatever he likes, declare undying love and all that, but if he treats you like shit, then where does that leave you? Hopefully, picking up the phone to ring him and dump him, realising that your mum was right after all ...

Girly luvved-up adventures

Things every girl should do with a lover at least once, and if
you're newly in lust then even better:

- 💜 Stay up all night and watch the sunrise
- 💜 Find a bar with a view and watch the sun set
- 💜 Go to Bondi Beach and watch the moon rise over the sea
  – magic!
- 💜 Spend all weekend in bed
- 💜 Have virtual sex in the park (as clean as you can make it
  for public viewing)
- 💜 Mind-sex (loads of looking and talking but no touching
  allowed)
- 💜 A mad weekend in New York City
- 💜 And still romantic – Paris in spring.

Help, my boyfriend is always making little remarks about my appearance, it really pisses me off - and makes me feel crap - what can I do?

Oh god, leave him!

Don't want to - you quite like him?

Oh well, it is time for girly tactics.

💜 If he has a tummy (pretty likely unless he's one of the ten men in the world who hasn't) stroke it often saying 'I do like you all cuddly like this ... You're so teddy-like and sweet.' Lay it on really thick.

💜 Bide your time honey, next time a gorgeous six-packed guy appears either in real life or on the TV say 'Blimey did you see that guy's stomach - he must spend a *lot of time* in the gym'

❤ Feel guilty for playing games with him?
Fear not – just because you're aware of what you're doing
doesn't make it any worse than him making comments about
your bum.

Commitment

What does it really mean?

You hear people banging on about it all of the time but what is it all about?

And do we really want it?

It is about deciding that you're in a relationship for the duration, for the long term. Meaning that every row you have is not a make or break one. That you can weather the ups and the downs but on balance it is a good relationship so you commit. It's a head thing.

When you're not committed you assess him constantly; where you keep a running tally in your head of good and bad stuff to decide whether he stays or he goes.

If you think he is a pain in the arse at times but you still love him anyway because there's a whole lot more to the relationship than some irritating habits then that's commitment.

Top 10 turn offs

1 inviting your mother wherever you go
2 not wanting to let him out of your sight
3 talking in a girly, baby voice
4 obsessing about your body
5 wearing full make up to bed
6 constantly seeking reassurance and never believing it
   when he does pay a compliment
7 banging on about getting married when you're nowhere
   near that stage yet
8 calling him by his pet name when his mates are around
9 making scenes to get attention
10 being insanely jealous.

Dilemma – how do I raise the subject of moving in?

Wait – maybe it's not a good idea if:

- 💜 you have only known each other for a few months
- 💜 your lease is up and it seems a convenient idea
- 💜 he's just moved out from living with another woman
- 💜 he still wants to spend most of his time with his mates
- 💜 he's a slob around the house
- 💜 he can't and won't cook
- 💜 you are his first girlfriend.

I think he's the one for me – how can I get him to commit?

For God's sake don't mention the 'c' word – commitment, that is, not the other rude word for girly bits. It bores men to death when girls go on about it. Men, otherwise known as creatures

who think differently from us, don't have the faintest clue what we're on about but panic and think we want to get married and have babies immediately. Maybe that is what you want – it is OK, they want the same thing really – but eventually – it just shocks them to hear their girlfriend say it out loud.

Marriage

How do I know he is the right one for me?

You can't be totally certain I'm afraid as love is not an exact science. Check your gut feeling – does he make you feel good? Do you enjoy your time together? Can you imagine having babies with him? Really? Would you rather be with him than anyone else?

If you're not under 25 then go for it.

How can I stop my boyfriend from flirting?

It is a tough one – tackle him about it and tell him how much it
bothers you. He is probably desperately unsure of his
attractiveness and needs constant reassurance. You could try
to give him an extra bit of love and confidence-boosting
support but it'd probably be like trying to put out a house fire
by peeing on it. Some men are just bottomless pits for love and
attention. Better to say it bores you and as much as you adore
him you'll not put up with it if he doesn't stop.

Is it possible to be passionate and monogamous? I worry that I'll get bored having sex with the same man and want to wander

- 💜 Make an effort to go away for dirty weekends.
- 💜 Take the lead.
- 💜 Have sex outdoors.
- 💜 Vary your habits – if you always do it at night, pounce on him in the middle of the day.
- 💜 Indulge in some discreet public fondling.
- 💜 When you're out whisper something naughty in his ear and sit back and watch the steam rise.

Men - What are they good for?

The pros and cons of having a boyfriend:

PROS

- 💜 cuddles
- 💜 they're usually stronger than us so they can carry bags
- 💜 warmth in bed
- 💜 regular and free orgasms
- 💜 dirty weekends
- 💜 they take you out to dinner on your birthday
- 💜 they're nice to look at

CONS

- 🖤 they take up too much space in bed
- 🖤 they want to know where you're going
- 🖤 they object if you want to go on holiday with the girls
- 🖤 they're time-consuming
- 🖤 they often want to see you on a Saturday night
- 🖤 you can't chat anyone else up (well …)
- 🖤 they would object if you slept with another boy

Girly games

It's not rocket science this dating game – it's much more complex than that.

Feeling taken for granted, ignored, feel as though you do all of the chasing? Now is the time to introduce some girly confusion. It will really make him stand back and think if you pay him loads of attention and tell him:

you're the best ...

you've got the biggest ...

no-one has ever done it like that to me before ...

this is the best night of my life ...

And – then don't call or return calls for a week and when he finally gets you on the phone, act surprised and pleased but almost as if you'd forgotten he existed.

He'll have gone through a whole range of emotions from flattered, cocky and very sure of you and then confused and wondering why you haven't called and what he should do next and will call you constantly.

Result! Game over – well played!

Does he really care? He probably does if:
- 💜 he turns up when he says he will
- 💜 he calls when he says he will
- 💜 he remembers your birthday
- 💜 he listens to you

I can't get my bloke to 'commit'

Commitment is a dirty word.

If you find yourself having a 'commitment' conversation then the cool, hard truth is probably that the guy you're with isn't as into you as you are into him. If you find yourself saying you want commitment – stop! You're flogging a dead horse.

Better to step away a little, cool it for a while and see what happens. Sounds like game-playing or manipulation – hello! – what do you think is going on when you bang on about commitment?

Sometimes I wonder why we keep on going out together ...

If you're confused, there is a way to find out whether it is worth keeping going. Firstly, don't expect everything to be perfect. A relationship is a mix of ups and downs, highs and lows and hopefully lots of ins and outs too. Instead of focussing on what is wrong in the relationship, concentrate on what you like about him; changing your routine even in small ways can get you out of a rut; make more effort than usual. If after a month you still find it tough and realise the relationship is making you miserable, put your energy into moving on.

Girly no-brainer

Do all guys like sexy underwear?

Are you kidding ... some like it better than others but all of them enjoy it. Try him out!

How do you know when you're in love?

It's hard to tell as most of us confuse love with lust. Lust is what gets you interested in the first place; I guess love must be what happens when you're not constantly wanting to fall into bed but you still want to be with him anyway.

Girly warning – love is not to be confused with couch potato domesticity where you slob around watching TV and eating fast food together because it's easier than going out.

Sex tips for long-term love

Keep doing it like you did when you first met – you might feel you can't be bothered, but once you get going it's worth it.

It's like any exercise, the more you do it, the more you get into it and enjoy it.

Don't forget to keep telling him how gorgeous he is, in bed and out.

Girly wake-up call

Whining and banging on about your appearance is boring and most of all to men – who generally couldn't care less about the details.

He's such a jealous guy

He goes mad if I ever dance with another guy, it's really embarrassing and unnecessary ...

You just have to ignore him. If your conscience is clear and you're not doing anything to make him feel left out, like ignoring him all night and flirting with every other man in the room, then you just tell him to sort it out – it's his problem. The key thing being that you are not going to change and start living like a nun, so he has to change if he wants to be with you.

Sorted girly
Don't knock the competition, it just makes you look like a bitch or seriously insecure. The hard, cold truth is that if he really wants to run off with someone else, you can't stop him anyway.

I always seem to get the jealous guys …

Ask yourself honestly – do you deep down enjoy him being
jealous and creating a scene because it makes you feel loved?
It's your life, but seriously it's worth breaking the pattern. Get
therapy now!

I'm so jealous of his ex I can't bear it …

As hard as you might find it, you need to be cool about his ex-
girlfriends. Exs are as much a part of life as periods and smear
tests, so get used to them – but you don't have to like them.

Remind yourself: he's going out with you not her; they're in
the past, you are the present.

Phone sex

With mobiles and txting and email it is easy to forget how sexy long, late night calls are – you gas about everything under the sun and you are subtly turning each other on, intensified by not being able to have each other. So pour yourself a drink, turn the lights down low, put on some mood music and give him a call.

BUT

If he's not home, don't torture yourself imagining where he is and what he's doing – put the lights on, crank up a dance tune and bounce on the sofa instead.

I really get the hump when he says 'yes' if I ask 'Does my bum look big in this?'

Don't ask the question. If you want a sound opinion ask your mates – after all what do blokes know about our standards.

Sex in the morning

Not only does it give you a rosy glow, it puts a smile on your face, makes you think about sex all day and inspires you to have a repeat performance that night.

Girly bonus: you'll be lost in your own world, but if you look about you'll notice more men than usual checking you out – they can sense you've been at it – which has the effect of making you feel even more sexy.

Girly last resort

Hey, if it doesn't work out, at least these days there is a money-back guarantee or way out – you can divorce . Divorce isn't nice or easy and no-one really wants to do it, but isn't it better than being stuck like women used to be?

Girly no-no

Don't start buying and leaving bridal mags around the house until you've set a date.

Dumping

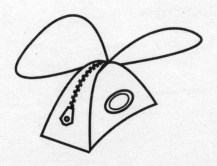

How will I survive?

Know your danger times – you need your friends when: you've been out on the lash and you just know you'll call your ex when you get home, leaving a string of messages, starting off with telling him how much you miss him and ending with abuse and/or sobbing.

The antidote: build a mental picture – imagine him coming back to his flat with a woman and them both, with horrified expressions, listening to your hysterical, pissed-up messages.

I feel like changing my look now that I'm free and single again

Never ever get a drastic haircut after you've been dumped – it could make things a whole lot worse. Go on a shopping spree instead (one that you can afford). Indulge yourself by having beauty treatments and massages.

Leave the haircut until you feel over him.

Saturday night survival blues

It is essential to book up at least the first month of Friday and Saturday nights after splitting up. Don't go anywhere you know will be full of couples – that rules out the pictures. If you are fresh out of love don't do it to yourself – you'll drop your popcorn in horror, as you'll be the only girl in there not snuggling up to a bloke.

Sometimes singles joints can depress you too by giving you that 'back on the meat market' feeling. Do something different instead – visiting a friend at the coast or in the countryside is the thing to do – with plenty of fresh air, long walks and no chance of bumping into your ex.

There's a good chance you'll get dumped if you:

- 💔 get caught in bed with someone else
- 💔 get put in jail
- 💔 have someone else's baby
- 💔 get fat because you can't be bothered any more
- 💔 never want to go out
- 💔 expect your boyfriend to go on family holidays
- 💔 do a striptease in your local pub – when your boyfriend isn't there...
- 💔 stick your hand down his brother's trousers
- 💔 send a filthy text message meant for another guy to him by mistake

Girly get-through it

OK, you've been dumped, you loved him to bits and you don't know how you're going to get through without him. You can have your night of self-pity – get all of your cushions and pillows on the sofa, put on your comfy leeei-sure suit, pour yourself a generous glass of white wine, sing at the top of your lungs and cry your heart out to these songs:

Top ten songs to sing when you've been dumped

1 Love Don't Live Here Any More – Rose Royce
2 Nothing Compares to U – Sinead O'Connor
3 (I want you) Back 4 Good – Take That
4 Yesterday – The Beatles
5 I Will Always Love You– Whitney Houston
6 Careless Whisper – George Michael
7 You Can Make Me Whole Again – Atomic Kitten
8 I Hate u So Much Right Now – Kellis
9 Survivor – Destiny's Child
10 I Will Survive – Gloria Gaynor

Revenge is sweet
But make it short, shift your focus away from him – and what he has done wrong – and onto yourself. Don't get hung up about it, don't get bitter, get on with your life and make it good.

Ready to get up and do it all again?

When you finally stop blubbing, rise from the sofa, dry your eyes and dress to kill, here's your next playlist for getting you out of the house and in the mood for kicking ass all over again:

1 Dancing Queen – Abba
2 Respect – Aretha Franklin
3 Hey Big Spender – Shirley Bassey
4 Pull Up to My Bumper Baby – In Your Long Black Limousine – Grace Jones

5   That's the Way uh huh uh huh I Like It – KC and the Sunshine Band
6   Club Tropicana – Wham
7   Girls Just Wanna Have Fun – Cindy Lauper
8   Groove is in the Heart – Dee-lite
9   I'm Coming Up – Pink
10 It's Raining Men – Geri

What's the best way to cope if you're on the rebound?

Take it easy and hold back a bit, don't be in a rush to get into something new. Make sure you have fun, get about a bit and don't get into a new relationship too soon.

If he's on the rebound

If he is on the rebound, assume he will be doing the same or should be doing it. If you force him into a relationship too soon, you'll end up with someone who felt they didn't have a proper break between their ex and you, and they might leave you to get it out of their system.

Help! I just can't seem to get over him ...

Check your self-talk:

If you're spending all day long saying in your head – 'God, I'm so lonely, I'll never get another bloke, I can't live without him' – well

it's not surprising you feel sad and sorry for yourself. Have a good cry, punch the pillows, roll around on your bed and then call your mates to arrange a cheer-up drink – moan as much as you like and then after that night try to think of yourself as out of despair and in recovery.

Use the brainwashing technique described earlier to get yourself in the right state of mind to get back out there on the scene again.

Help, I am going to get dumped if I'm late and leave him waiting one more time ...

Don't be daft – you don't need to be on time, you just need some damn fine excuses!

- 💜 I had to drive around looking for a chemist that was open so I could buy some tampons
- 💜 I had to work late. Heh heh, always a good one!
- 💜 The cat vomited all over the bed just as I was about to leave.
- 💜 My best friend found out her boyfriend was having an affair (it helps if he doesn't know her)
- 💜 My gran called and she never sees anyone but the postman and so I had to stay and chat...

or

If you're really stuck blame it on public transport or your car breaking down.

Make your revenge short and sweet

Piss him off and forget him.

If he dumps you – get your friends to club together to rent for a day the car he's always lusted after but could never afford. Drive where you know he'll see you and then zoom off to cruise and forget him!

Moral dilemmas

I think my boyfriend might be cheating on me – how can I really tell?

Warning signs include:

- 💔 being unavailable
- 💔 changes in tastes and habits
- 💔 suddenly wearing new pants
- 💔 wearing aftershave when he never has before
- 💔 whistling a lot for no apparent reason
- 💔 his mates seem to avoid you or they flirt with you when usually they never would
- 💔 he is uncomfortable when his mates are around (he thinks they'll give him away)
- 💔 he suddenly acts like a different man in bed
- 💔 he goes to the corner shop more often (to make a call to her).

I think my man is still in love with his ex – he is always going on about her. What can I do?

Ask him as calmly as you can if what you fear is true – preparing yourself for a 'yes' or a 'no' answer.

Have your mates on standby with tea and sympathy or wine and fags in case of a 'yes' answer.

If you must two-time, make sure you don't get caught by acting differently with your boyfriend

Don't:

- ♥ be too nice
- ♥ wear new and sexier undies
- ♥ sing in the shower when you never have before
- ♥ suddenly start doing new things in bed
- ♥ ever get his name wrong.

I really don't want to go out tonight but he asked me ages ago – how can I blow him out without seeming a bitch?

- 💜 your washing machine has flooded and you have to wait for the plumber
- 💜 your gran needs you (mmm her again)
- 💜 a long lost friend from Australia has turned up as a surprise
- 💜 your cat is being repeatedly sick all over the house.

We had a row and it was all my fault – I'm bored of him being cross, so how do I make it up?

Roll out the old classic – PMS.

If you don't suffer from it, you do now.

Cheating Bastard

I thoroughly recommend slapping the guilty pair if you find
them together – you'll always regret the missed opportunity if
you don't. If you are truly against violence (sigh!), then treat
them like rutting dogs – drenching them with a bowl of water
will soon split them apart.

(Don't forget she might be an innocent party, he may have
told her he was single, so take it out on him.)

Whether you split and go your separate ways or you decide
to forgive and forget, the memory of giving them a good shock
will give you a story to dine out on and warm you in your
darkest and loneliest moments.

I don't get it – we are really good together, why did he cheat on me?

Well, if you've never done it before there's the buzz of illicit sex, sex without ties or responsibility can make you feel really alive and powerful.

And it's not just a bloke thing either.

Should I forgive him and give him a second chance?

It could go either way:

He might be so terrified at your reaction and the fear of losing you that he'd never stray again.

OR he might feel pleased that he got away with it and do it again.

It's your call but one thing is for sure, he doesn't deserve a third chance if there is a next time.

I'm cheating on my bloke and I just can't stop

You don't really want to give it up if you 'can't'.

   If you're happy, fine – just be aware that you could be dumped by your boyfriend if he finds out. If that wouldn't bother you too much, why are you bothering to keep him on anyway – sack him!

I really fancy my friend's ex – he's now made a move – what to do?

All's fair in love and war – the only exception is if she is obviously still in love with him or if he treated her terribly. In those two instances I would forget him – especially if it is only lust. But if it was a cool split, then what are you waiting for – just tell your friend before she hears it from someone else.

Girly no no's
Don't ever beg him to come back – he probably won't – and it'll always make you cringe once you're over him.
If he does come back it will never be equal again.

Oh my giddy aunt – he caught me out with another guy – how am I going to get out of this one?

The number one rule if you are going to mess around with two guys at the same time is that at least one of them must know the truth. That way if things do turn out disastrously and both guys happen to be in the same place at the same time and running away is not an option, then at least the one who is in the know will play along with whatever daft excuse you come up with.

Favourite lies if you get caught:

John, meet my cousin Sam.
Fred, I've always wanted you to meet my old school pal Michael.
David, meet my stepfather – yes my mum is a bit of a toy boy freak.

EMBARRASSING SCENARIOS

I walked in on my boyfriend playing with himself – how does one react?

If you feel really uncomfortable about it, sneak away without him seeing you or make lots of noise in the hallway, giving him time to compose himself.

If you're cool about it – tease him about it but make the most of what has arisen – ask if he needs a hand and get involved!

Girly honesty

Don't try to save your conscience by telling him about your squeeze on the side. If you want to keep your boyfriend rather than the other guy, keep it as your guilty secret even if it makes you feel bad. You've had your fun, now take the guilt like a big girl.

Oops! I got caught with my hand down my pants

If you get caught yourself, there are only two approaches:
be bold and brazen – come and finish me off, baby;
blag your way out of it – pretend to be applying thrush cream –
enthusiastically – the very thought will put any idea that you
were having solo sex totally out of his mind.

Conclusion

Don't forget you only live once, and your job is to enjoy it.

Have safe sex, have fun, don't put up with a bastard, don't act like a cow.

Don't love half-heartedly.

When you're in love, love fully, passionately and deeply. Don't waste time by holding back – yes you might get hurt but that's life – you'll get over it.

And lastly, don't leave this book lying around where blokes can see what you're up to ...

the Handbag Book of Girly Emergencies

"If you're a hot chick who likes to party hard you need this book"
OK Magazine

Order further titles from your local bookshop, or have them
delivered direct to your door by Bookpost

Catalogue Man	£7.99	☐
the Ann Summers little book of sex	£5.99	☐
the Handbag Book of Girly Emergencies	£5.99	☐

FREE POST AND PACKING
Overseas customers allow £2 per paperback

PHONE: **01624 677237**

POST: **Random House Books**
c/o Bookpost, PO Box 29, Douglas
Isle of Man, IM99 1BQ

FAX: **01624 670923**

EMAIL: **bookshop@enterprise.net**

CHEQUES AND CREDIT CARDS ACCEPTED
Prices and availability subject to change without notice
Allow 28 days for delivery
www.randomhouse.co.uk